T0199203

my
mini
creative colouring book

to

relax the mind

ROBYN J COURT

To order additional copies of this book, contact:
Xlibris
1-800-455-039
www.xlibris.com.au
Orders@Xlibris.com.au

CREATIVE WORKS

BY

ROBYN J COURT

Have
fun
Everyone

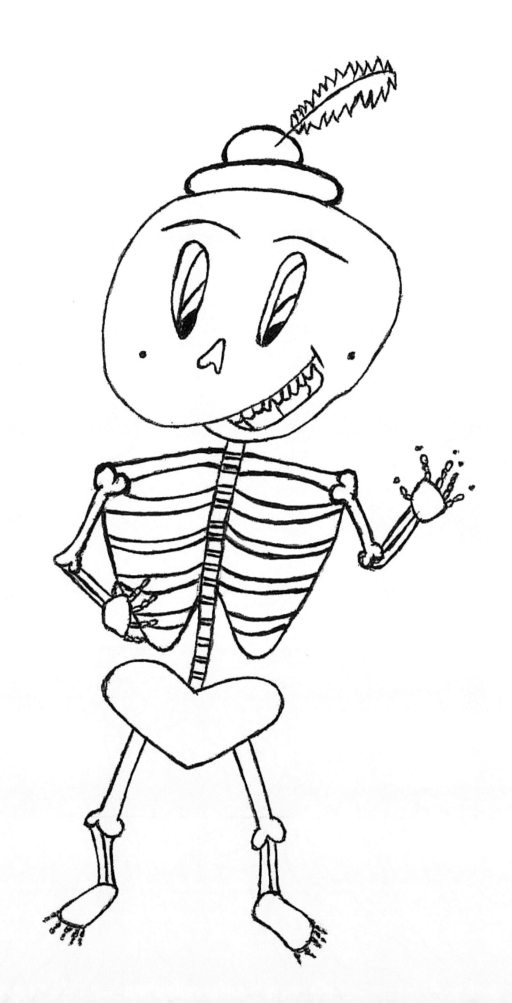

Printed in the United States
By Bookmasters